SAD
SUPERPOWER

Sad Superpower
Copyright © 2022 by *Todd French*

Published in the United States of America
ISBN   Paperback: 978-1-958030-31-8
ISBN   eBook: 978-1-958030-32-5

The opinions expressed by the author are not necessarily those of ReadersMagnet, LLC.

ReadersMagnet, LLC
10620 Treena Street, Suite 230 | San Diego, California, 92131 USA
1.619. 354. 2643 | www.readersmagnet.com

Cover design by *Kent Gabutin*
Interior design by *Dorothy Lee*

TABLE OF CONTENTS

CANADIAN GEESE

The Canadian geese from the park pass overhea
About 7:00pm or thereabouts each eve
In a loose v heading west or south-west
Long-necked leader in front short bill straining
Their undersides dabbed with shadow
While they raucously honker over well I don't know
I guess the remains of the goose day
The quality of the evening munch of
Stems seeds insects and bulbs
Or maybe some piece of avian hilarity
At the expense of the dour ibis or the flighty blue-white swallows
Who knows what sets a goose off or gives them the funnies
As long as it's not a joke at my expense or yours.

If I'm lucky and I'm inside and hear them coming
I can slip outside and stride briskly down the front walk
And catch them flying past my home gray white and black feathers
Limned in dusk's unstable mix of molten sun lather and calligraphy ink
Intent on the sky's violent peach and retiring blue
Then suddenly banking toward the sea
Their honking setting off the guard dog
Across the street who takes his job seriously
It's a rare pleasure to watch them wing away
As the dark takes the prunus trees and bougainvillea
Pours bit by bit like a good Gallo down the hibiscus
While the first crickets begin their tremolos
The monarchs and Harford's Sulphurs long gone
The honeybees and fiery skippers with them

If I'm unlucky they catch me at the bathroom mirror
When the sliding glass door is open
And I am standing there with my hair scissors
Chin at an angle squinting into the glass
Trying to remove the odd black whisker from the tidal white
That has taken my beard with celerity and dispatch
Not a bit of the old red-gold left
Not even a smidge like a last dollop of red bean paste on
The shaved ice and condensed milk of a Japanese Kakigori dessert
Or maybe I'm looking at the new wrinkles or skin-tag

Just to the right of my eye that wasn't there last year
The new mole on a sun-weathered patch of neck
That's when the Canadian geese get me
Their derisive gobblegot hitting home when I am trying
To stave off or inventory the sure marks of age or death
Looking for traces of the youth I used to be

No the humor isn't appreciated and I pause
Until their ragged gusts of mockery and brio recedes
And I imagine what they are saying
As I stand there sighing scissors in hand
We'll pass overhead today
We'll pass overhead tomorrow
As long as dusk follows day there will be geese from the park
Passing over the peak of your roof and down your block
There will be cricket chirrup and tremolo
Black phoebe bluebird and finch warble
There will be autumn leaves muttering their parchment lingo
As they cartwheel across cooling pavement asphalt and lawn
Rasp of pampas grass and beach-grass
Depend on it friend we'll pass by tomorrow
And the next day with a joke in our bills

But what about you?

LUCHADORS

Maybe the government will hire luchadors
To help us deal with responsible masking
A veritable flood of Santos, Infernos, Medicos,
Caras', Tiger Masks, Kings, Reys and Fantasticos
In flashy tights or business suits
Delivering presentations via Zoom from wrestling halls
School gymnasiums and town auditoriums
About how to be Opaque for The Greater Good
How to bear the slow bleed of social isolation
With a solid moonsault a frog splash or a plancha
To bounce back when we're blue with a flying surfboard
How to embrace the worst and keep from
Throwing out the script for a shoot
When constitutional intimations impinge
Maybe they'll help us ignore the hecklers
Shouting from the cheap-seats of our conscience
About crushed Amendments and possibilities
Provide us with pointers on executing

The fast scoot out under the bottom ring-rope
When the despair of our children compels us to
Cut the ties and fling the face into the crowd
Maybe we'll learn to stop loathing the governor
When he kicks back at the French restaurant/wine-bar
While health-inspectors close eateries
Catering to common sense and survival instinct
Or when the cops fold the gym owner into the cruiser
Perhaps the high-flyers will truly teach us the best way
To take the folding-chair to the back
The roll of quarters in a sock upside the head
The long count-out before the reversal of fortune
To just keep our peace and honor the mask
Accept the fast tag to loneliness
And bury hope beneath nylon and vinyl

ABRAHAM LABORIEL

When I hear Abraham Laboriel lay down that bass
I feel like I'm sitting in a lawn chair on that glass and fire sea
Watching him swat down a 10 nation army
Knocking jacinth and brimstone breastplates off
A 250 million east demon relief force
Like the ash and mud of the future world could
Funnel back up into fire maples and wisteria
The sky go back to its boiling robin blue
The clouds to poleaxed cumulus bears
Lark song and jay song pushing back the noon day dark
Listen to He is Exalted or Listen to Your Brother
And you'd think this world of baize and gold
Could go on forever (it won't but you feel like it could)
You'd feel like every spirit in the invisible realm
Was giddy as a kid grabbing a dog by the paws
Teaching it to dance

RETURNING THE TICKET TO TARSHISH

I wonder if Jonah ever returned that ticket to Tarshish
Did he keep the memory of it close like a skin of sour wine
Standing dismayed trembling over the worm-shriveled
Fly-spotted chunks of gourd cries of fasting
Freighting the air like a hard northeaster
When His voice faded from the air like the last
Sweet note of a kinnor made of almug and sheep gut
Love unwanted scrabbling at the lobes of the prophet's ears
Like some hissed-for bee or wasp
I wonder what Jonah did when mercy floated down
Like Peter's canopy on to the Assyrian hive
I can see him in the wreck of his reed-plaited booth
Hands opening and closing in impotent rage
Tatters of his brine and baleen-smelling robes
Whipping head dipped as if he was ready to ram it
Back into the whale's gums praying for the clasp of waves
Preferring abyssal depths to the totality of God's love.

I wonder if Jonah kicked the can back to Judah
The memory of forgiveness a stew of bad figs and quinces in his gut
Or did he stumble down to Nineveh teeth-clenched eyes blind
Half-hoping for the gift of chariot-squall
The repudiation of God's grace by Ashur's faith of steel
The bronze gate bands professing future victories and mutilations
The wink of medallions-one demon defending against another
Infernal malice spike upon spike like a crown of thorns starfish
Did he wish he could cut the throat of every lowing oxen
Every crying goat and bleating sheep

Or did Jonah's hard heart open like the wings of a young bird
Falling from the nest bouncing and jouncing on hard crags
Before taking to the balm of thermals and sun
When his eyes near-blind as a rhino's
Fastened on those of a ring-bearded warrior fluted helm askew
Sun-leeched features smeared with sackcloth
Kneeling under the flank of a winged bull
Holding his sobbing wife and child
Reed-thin with the conviction of fasting
Did Jonah set about the work of shelling the old heart
In his breast like a rotten walnut bit by stubborn bit

And truly dredge his soul from its pocket of whale's brush
Sea-grape gall and krill?

Will we let go of our ticket to Tarshish
When the Antifa child or Neo-Nazi
This generation of Call of Duty Sturmabteilung
Repent and turn their brimming gaze to us
And make their way from the frisking fire
Of their own implacable and pitiless Ashurs
Towards the awesome love and grace of God?

THANK YOU MY LITTLE PONY FRIENDSHIP

"My village was a sanctuary of equality, where nopony's cutie mark allowed them to feel superior! It was a special place, and you and your friends took it away! Now it's my turn to take something special from you! Without the rainboom, you and your friends will never form your special cutie mark bonds! Cutie marks for cutie marks! Sounds like a fair trade to me!"
~ Starlight Glimmer and her plan for revenge.

Before I could even talk to them about Marx, Mao and Stalin,
About the mounds of skulls, gulags and famine,
The reeducation camps, purges and executions,
The horrors of Mao's Great Leap, Stalin's starvation of the Ukrainians,
Pol Pot and the atrocities of the Khmer Rouge,
The Kim family and North Korea, the Viet-Cong.
My twin daughters informed me that they knew quite well
That communism was a force for evil on the earth,
They didn't need any history lessons from me,
Bethany and Victoria informed me they understood
How truly evil socialist systems are.
In My Little Pony Friendship, the dictatorial unicorn Starlight Glimmer
Uses her magic powers to steal everyone's cutie-mark,
Replacing it with an equal sign that inhibits their abilities.
I must explain that Starlight Glimmer is the purple-maned villain
Introduced in Season Five of My Little Pony.
"She wants everyone to be equal, except her!"
"Yeah, she was an absolute tyrant, dad!"
I marveled at this example of equine cartoon totalitarianism,
Wisdom from the gurus at Netflix,
And shook my head in bemusement as we drove home,
Trying my best-and succeeding-in not fuming about masks
And Mandates-my girls have heard it before.
Then we went back to the happy burble of the day,

The girls talking about new friends, the hang-out tree,
Coming up with a gift for their Egyptian girlfriend
Whom they have known since Middle School,
The bully from way back who seems to have reformed,
And isn't as bad looking as they once thought,
While Victoria showed me the new additions on her sketchpad.
Starlight Glimmer, I chuckled to myself.
Imagine that.
Imagine that.

ELKHORN SLOUGH/MOSS LANDING 5/30/21

The Caspian Tern pauses mid-air before diving
Into the slough's muddy olive waters and tangles of eel-grass
Flapping its white wings like a bat's fashioning them into
Fussy accordion pleats before it spears down
Sending up a brief spray of sun-shot beads of moisture
Resurfacing soon after some morsel wriggling in their orange bill
Black and ash-colored Brandt's and
Pelagic cormorants feed in the same area
Sartorial feather splendor of sober darks contrasting
with the tern's white and light grey
It's called Cooperative Feeding says our Elkhorn Slough Safari guide
Terns and cormorants are absolutely comfortable feeding side by side

In the shallows the snowy egret stilt-walks through the shore mud
As self-possessed as a tea-master of feudal Japan
Ignoring The Onin War raging outside his gate
Transfixed by porcelain the ephemerality of beauty
The snowy egret goes along its high-stepping way
With an astronaut's slow-mo moon-booted majesty
Occasionally turning its bright white head and long dark bill
Towards the raucous collective as if to say
Really now really
Does it require
Such a noisy effort?
Really now

I HARDLY RECOGNIZE YOU

My friend tell me is that really you
Looking as if you've been crawling
Through Polyphemus' sheep-folds spine bowed
From fear of the eye-slopped hoodwinked man-eater's hand
Relying on ride of ram-belly out into the light
Silent scream fed to the underside of filthy fleece
Spelunking through gnawed bone and fly blot to the blue beyond cave
Holding fast to some tear-bleared hope
Of tide and ship-prow gannet and tern cry
Fast slip through eel-grass and seaweed
How is it friend that care has brought
New runnels to your forehead rheum to the eye
Hair an autumn hayrick splashed with claret turning to vinegar
Did you sign on as keel-hand to some wave-slagged Aeneas
Banking on reaching Latium's harbor and a new home
Hills browed with chaplets of green vine and black grape
Only to find an angry Turnus swearing cuirass and sword
Where did you go friend that I find you changed
Slat-ribbed and grizzled as a spurned yellow dog
Shivering as if your way has wended too long nightside
Moon rind Arroyo cold and bat-cloud for company
Blanket-wrapped exigencies down to old coals and potsherds
Tell me friend where have you gone that you look so worn
As sea-glass or a ghost of wasp-paper in a strong blow
Where did you go friend what inhospitable land
Or bristling quay's repulsion has brought you to this

Friend I went nowhere
I was here all along
It is my nation that has become a stranger to me

FAUCI'S EMAILS

June gloom I am up early
Massacring weeds in the back planter
Hanging tail-up on its tether
The crow decoy
Stirs in the breeze

LOAVES AND FISHES

The Sad Super Power needs a loaves and fishes day
I want to sit on a green hill under twilight's rose and mandarin tussle
And see tribalism rage and hate dissolve beneath the pungent aromas of
Barbels musht and fresh bread while The Son of Man
Shares The Beatitudes with us and claps Peter on the back afterwards
Reminding him and all of us how the gospels ended with a fish-fry
Forgiveness and reconciliation on the shores of Galilee
Fishers of Men turned Fishers of Fish then back again
Doubt dead as the black eye of the biny on the coals
I want to recline with several of my worst enemies
Separating past hurts and enmities like smoking flesh from
A tilapia's mini-marimba rack of rib
Flicking the crumbs to the pismires and evening hoppers
Tossing the heads to the low-strafing tight-banking swallows
And take in the chatter of people happy to cleanse their palate
Of searchlight and sentry sentiment gruel and gristle
Asking one another in the dwindling light
How do we find mercy define it share it in the highways and byways
Of Florida or Portland Minnesota how do we comfort one another
Lord what I would give to hear that dialogue open like a
Big furred clam to a skindiver's knife the pearl for the taking
Yes I would give my right hand to feel the feather-tease of long grass
Take in the soul's home-smell of evening primrose and Mordechai
The concrete milkshake tossers and militiamen grooving together
The melanin content hucksters and patriots parsing it out
The CNN and Fox reporters offering to bring each other seconds
Of the miraculously multiplied chow
Pant cuffs rolled up skirts grass-stained no hand craving a mic
God's promises to the meek the peacemakers the justice-seekers
Laughing at someone's new ewe kicking up a fuss
Kids playing keep away with a shepherd's staff
Ruffling the dog's neck as it noses for scraps

Laughing at the goat chewing the back of a t-shirt
Love bridging the gaps like old strangler vines across
A chasm in some fun Saturday morning serial
Hero swinging forward bit by bit ignoring bat funnel
Spear rain from above the figure-eights of river 'gators below
It would be great to see the people in the Sad Super Power
Hash it out warmed by the Son of God's soliloquy
Hearts hard as diamond and corundum opening opening like poppy cups
The end of the country's Blues and Greens chariot faction fracas
Loud belches class clown cut-ups joshing and elbow bumps
I wish we could have that fish-fry bellies full souls full
The dead sorrows and divisions going into the leftover baskets
The first stick-pin glints of evening's shining
Down on sanity and goodwill largesse and first trust
I wish we could have
That day of loaves and fishes

EX-MILITARY DOGS ON THE NIGHT OF THE FOURTH OF JULY

I just hope there is someone holding a trembling flank
Providing a shoulder for the press of a scarred muzzle
A comrade sitting under a table holding and gentling
Their buddy trembling at each star-fall of light
Rapport and cannonade turning the block into a war-zone
I hope someone a man or woman is hugging their friend
Who remembers a moon-lit dash across a palm field
Towards an insurgents base in Mahmudiyah or Fallujah
Who remembers the chatter of AKS-74u Makarov pistol IED
Being assisted over the sagging strands of razor-wire
Friends friends friends falling to the right and left while bodies
Boiled out of sheds and bomb-pocked ruins
Faces kerchiefed in black or white short sleeves or robes
Wind and bullet-tugged in the trade-off of arms
Barrels barking friends barking dogs barking
Later sniffing for IEDs on the roadside in the 104 heat
Pulled up short on a leash when one of the lead convoy vehicles
Went up in a noon-star flash of fire and metal
Blood smell metal scent bird scent fear scent anger smell everywhere
Children on the shoulder burying their faces in the
Black and dusty folds of their mothers burkhas

I hope there's someone in the back room of the house
Stroking the brindled or gray head of the dog they redeemed
Or brought home from the war-fields refusing to part
Speaking soft words until
The thunder stops
And
The
Sun
Comes
Out

THIS ISN'T WHO WE ARE

The snap of a fish-chum breeze
Last dead shivers of shark scirocco
Winding around the statue's pissed on pedestal
Snaking its way through half-charred hanks
Of local biz and major chain cardboard beg
PLEASE DON'T LOOT US WE SUPPORT BLM
WE ARE INCLUSIVE PLEASE DON'T LOOT
Whining through rifts of PD windshield particles
Tearing tear-gas fog into gray-yellow rags
Prowling over chunks of stomped concrete lattes
Sending abandoned Black Bloc masks sky-loft
Like swarms of moon and comb jellies
Muttering the same sad defeated query
Long after you have left
And the law-abiding picking through burnt shops
Cursing The Church of Night as Catalyst
The mercies of a metastasis of hoodies

Alright, then tell us, who are we?

COFFEE SHOP CLOCK 08/27/21

I was in a local coffee shop that honors the armed forces
And I paused my morning cup of joe halfway to my lips
To look at the small round scarlet clock on the wall across the way
The skittering florescent light jounced off its glass bubble
Noticed the highlighted hours which were marked as golden chevrons
The clock seemed to me a single drop of blood flicked from the wound
Of some ancient hero if heroes were thirty feet tall
Wore helmets of hallowed out granite and marl fog-kissed rain-kissed
And bore uprooted oaks and firs for swords
A mile or so of bear and lion skins for armor
And I thought of other heroes blood dearly spent at that very moment
In Kabul at the airport by men and women of this nation
I saw a young mother in her ACU and MultiCam
Her M16 or M249 in hand body-armor dusted with sand
And her war-face stretched tight as she shouted instructions
To the panicked populace foreign nationals one hand waving
Standing between a screaming child and
the anthropoid bare and bloody minimum
I saw someone's father someone's brother someone's sister
Making a breach for an ally an interpreter young woman in a burka
Already imagining the chains and smelling stale pistachio and grease
On the hands of her future rapist//half-hour Talban husband
As I looked over at the blood clock and the golden chevrons
My mind reflected on valor courage skill honor brotherhood
That could only be valor courage skill honor brotherhood
Not matter how betrayed forsaken abused misused
Like sea-coast ernes their wings clipped tossed into cruel swells
Still wielding beak and claw against gray water and gust
While old doddering fishermen laughed at the transom
Taking their cues from punch-drunk cormorants
I can't say more
I don't trust myself to say more

23

How can anyone say more
So I drank my coffee and looked at the clock's gold chevrons
And thought of chevrons and blood spent that moment that second
By madmen in The Oval Office taking their orders
from punch-drunk cormorants
Blood and chevrons suspended in the heat-hammered scream-bright air
And I prayed I prayed my God to my God
to watch over them and their charges
I prayed to God to look on valor courage skill
brotherhood life laid down for another
And to have mercy to have mercy to be shield buckler saving hand
Isaiah 41: "those who war against you will be nothing at all
For I, The Lord your God, hold your right hand"
And I prayed please God them out of this
Roman Crassus Carrhae hell
While there is still time

PORTUGUESE MAN O' WAR

Bit by bit summer's heat is breaking up
Like a Portuguese Man o' War jellyfish
Canceled by committee
On a barely breathing sea

NINEVITES

Still reeling from the horrors of Afghanistan the fires in my state
The destruction wrought by hurricane Ida Antifa teachers
Force-feeding communism down the throats of kids
Failing cities tides of homeless and breached borders
Dismayed and saddened at how swiftly The Sad Superpower is falling
I half feel like confronting the ghosts of Jonah's Ninevites
(I know bad didn't bring King Saul a lick
of good when he summoned Samuel)
The ring-bearded warriors fluted helms on their heads
Faces opaque to compassion as the commandments of Ashur
Mercy thin as the dust-sprays between chariot wheels
Really I want to ask them tell me what made you change
Win a 100-year stay of execution before another messenger served notice
Was it really the baleen-stinking fish-spat prophet's street-preaching?
He couldn't have delivered The Lord's warning with much relish
His commission's outreach hissed through
teeth bared like a rhesus monkey
It's shaved head studded with electrodes trailing wires
It's not like Jonah was afire with The Baptist's fervor calling you
To shed your sins in the sweet waters of the Khosr, yes?
No, the three-day fish-belly shake made Jonah get the lead out
But with little love-you couldn't coax love for the enemy from him
Anymore than you could expect granite and shale to
Produce a single rose or a bouquet of orchids
A wolf-dame whelping a lamb in her den
He strode through the city eyes jonesing for black cloud and fire gout
Hoping for life smoothed out to pulverized plain of black glass
How is it that you the crucifiers the
mutilators dismemberers lion-stranglers
Nation smashers eunuch makers chiselers
of Ashurbanipal's atrocity murals
One eye on spear and shield the other on the demon-haunted sands

Wall-eyed for the Uttuku Alu and Gallu ass-teeth bull-body or wing
(How could you not be demon-haunted with so much blood and cruelty)
Necks rubbed raw by the thongs of demon amulet upon demon amulet
How is it that you-al of you-bought a reprieve from The Lord?
I am looking at my country which truth told was kinder than yours
In its founding its principles its mission shining beacon on the hill
And I am far too pessimistic to believe we will have a shot
At a Nineveh Moment ash-cloth for all three branches of government
President Biden and VP Harris sitting in ashes Mitch and Chuck fasting
The Squad shinnying up stone pedestals like a plethora of Stylus'
So I want to ask you bloody-minded Sons of Ashur
What made you listen to the reluctant servant of Jehovah
What mix of bad astronomy drought and famine brought you to that
point?
I see nothing in your murals to suggest repentance's balms
Cairns of heads and limbs bloody overthrown Manasseh hook in his nose
Banded in bronze (coming to repentance in your dungeons!)
Hornet-nest of bloody-handed soldiers when did you look
At the oil and bitumen spring of your awful hearts
And say to yourselves we have gone far enough and no further?
The Sad Superpower could use a word, gentlemen
Now while we still have time

SHAMSIA HASSANI

I will admit that as bad as the film footage is of the people
Clutching on to the underside of plane transports
The Christians fleeing to the mountains tweeting that the
Taliban have said they know who they are and are coming for them
The female mayor of Kabul resigning herself to death
I am haunted by the graffiti painting of this young woman
Afghan street artist Shamsia Hassani who applies
Swirling hues to bomb-pocked sections of wall
Hope Love and Understanding proffered in the pale corona
Of potted blooms from the hands of young girls
Dashed to the ground by slate-gray fighters offering
In turn the anthropoid minimum of the human soul
My mind returns again and again to her work Nightmare
The young girl long-lashed in parted light blue burka
In the foreground eyes downcast red heart on her chest
Keyboard hugged tight to her chest crazy-tilt outlines
Of buildings on her skirt and behind her in shadowy picket
Looming like an implacable mountain range
In black and charcoal Taliban soldiers
Faces adamantine to one hammered piton of pity

And I wonder now where is she now
Is she on the run is she in hiding or even alive
Paint cans alley tossed abandoned dancing skittering
In the wake of speeding jeeps and armor-gridded trucks
Even now is blind ignorance hate-driven fanaticism
Whitewashing or pick-axing away the smudge of a face
The red of a kerchief the snow white lick of a thistle
Drifting like an invitation to a stalagmite figure
Gray as ibis a hob's slit of scarlet for an eye
Promising the end of all future blooms

THE WOMEN AND GIRLS OF AFGHANISTAN

Beneath the rubble and ordnance mound
Beneath shredded boas of battle smoke
The bunting in its buried cage
Forgets its song

"PRESENT"

"Yes, I wept. I wept at the complete lack of care for the human beings that are impacted by these decisions, I wept at an institution choosing a path of maximum volatility and minimum consideration for its own political convenience."
—Congresswoman Alexandria Ocasio-Cortez to her constituents on Twitter

The congresswoman from New York serving The Sad Superpower
Decided to vote "Present" rather than "yes" or "no"
On whether to pass $1 billion in the House of Representatives
To replenish the nation of Israel's Iron Dome missile defense system
Following the latest terrorist attacks by Hamas.
I don't know why she didn't just let her "nay be a nay,"
But she chose to vote "present" instead of a simple "No."
She had castigated colleague Tulsi Gabbard for voting "Present"
When it came to impeaching President Trump,
So, I don't know what to say.
Her sibilant sisterhood had no problems assaying a "Nay."

Then she repented-yes, she repented that she couldn't stop
The aid package from passing and saving much life.
Her conscience was a black eel-scramble in her guts
It was a flensing knife to her sensibilities and soul.

She repented and apologized.

And she released the waterwork-ah my plebes she let the tears flow.
The impertinent notion that Jews, Arabs, Druze and Christians
Wouldn't wise up and just go along with being blown to bits
By the constant barrages of thousands of Hamas rockets
Provoked her to a such depths of heart-rending lachrymosity
That the crocodiles of the Nile would have croaked, "you go, sister,"

Honest, it would have wrung freshets of sympathetic tears from
Every statue of the demon Pazuzu left standing in Assyria/Modern Iraq.
The uttukus, Gallus, Lilus and Alus-the worst of Nergal's worst
The doleful and suppurating cadres of the lower world
Would have flooded the wastes with their shared grief.
The Rephaim and Nephilim would have screed and keened
Like the black-winged kites and dark chanting goshawks.
They wouldn't have been unmoved but fanned their burnt black wings.
They would have stood shoulder-to-shoulder
With The Crying Congresswoman-Legion would have cried.

Not one devil in hell would have had a dry eye.
The idea that little children little babies toddlers children
Sobbing in fall-out shelters hiding under beds
Curled fetal under beds pushing themselves further into
Their father mother brother sister's chests and chins
Traumatized eyes on firelight frisk on atomized glass stone and plaster
Blast-splintered window-frames and nails
Praying for the explosions and klaxons of sirens to die.
The idea that Jewish children would want to go on live on
Wouldn't just opt to perish under a hail of terrorist hate and death
Was just too much for the sensitive miss to contemplate.
The quark star of her heart and soul collapsed at the idea.
Humanity's hydration went dry as driftwood
Transformed into the desert's checkerboard of alkaline and salt.
She needed comfort from her colleagues.
She needed to frame her apologies on Twitter
Where the right and left would be whittling their knives.
Did we have hearts of granite or feldspar?
Who wouldn't have shared her tears?
Were we as opaque to pain as chisel-grooved and runneled gargoyeles?

She didn't cry for Afik, 4, killed on his playground
By rockets, or for Yuval, 4 or Dorit, 2. Who died on the streets
During the attacks...but she cried.

If the ghost of the Moabite King Balak who lost a mint
On his prophet-for-hire Balaam when the latter blessed the Jews
At the command of The Lord instead of cursing the migrating tribes
As he had been instructed and paid to do
Could have been furled out of hell to attend that session of the House
I have no doubt whatsoever he would have comforted
The crying congresswoman from New York
Would have pressed his downturned ectoplasmic lips
Reeking of gall wormwood and bitumen to her ear
And whispered, "Hey, believe me, I know just how you feel."
"I walked around my palace for days whipped like a dog and
Taboring like a dove when that religious hack Balaam
And his stupid donkey let me down."

GRAND CANYON/NORTH RIM, AZ 08/10/21

When my oldest daughter balked at walking out
On to the (fenced) spit of stone overlooking the gorge
Of the Grand Canyon's North rim early on in our tour
I simply said Here I Am We Can Both Do It Here I Am
Here I Am Right Behind You Let's Do It
And we assayed the look-out point unsteady as passengers
On a plane weaving drunk-wise during a sharp bank
Whalers/Sharkers edging to the front of the ship's pulpit
Shellacked by sea-thunder and gannet sky's downpour
That's a fair approximation of how it felt
I hated heights as much as she did
We made it to the very end stone ledge and chain
God's gracious gravity balm and anchor
She took her photos hand steady while the twins cheered
And her mother looked on in pride
There we stood perched under the guileless blue
Triremes and biremes of cumulus scudding by
While darker clouds mumbled behind us
And ravens slumming the thermals around us
Circling dropping fringed wings fluttering
Below us profundity denying profundity a voice
Dizzying drops and heights of limestone sandstone and sediment
Horizontal bands of washed-out incarnadine and yellow and green
Dotted with the infinitesimal green of ponderosa pine and scrub
Better poets than I have used metaphors for faith and chasm
But still and all as the masked and unmasked passed by us
In spite of the pandemic scares and vagaries of politics and virology
Fear of heights or fear of blights bodies in motion
Needed the community of bodies in motion
Countering nature's salvos at our significance with
Some shared internal contract with the solidity of rock rail and link
Some belief that God loves us enough to take us up

The un-railed/un-fenced paths and back
A chance to drop our fears into the yawning gulf below
Sure we were proof against caroming rock rain's wash-out
Trail-earth's tilt misstep slide and fall
And here was the antidote and awe capping the lid
On the frog-pot squirm of worries and chafes
No lockdowns no shelter-in-place no mandates
Observed by the complicity of stone and sky
My oldest daughter took the last of her photos
And walked with sure steps from the promontory
And we headed ever upwards

SORRY BUT I AM STILL NOT USED TO DISTANCE ARROWS

Sorry but I am still not used to distance arrows
The Covid warning stickers on the store floors instructing us
To stay six feet back from the next shopper in the check-out line
They give me a chill because I find myself equating
Six feet back to six feet under the parlance of grave and dirt
Isolation of wreath and box surety of shovel scrape and sod fall
And in the same way I see death by degrees cold ice crackle
Of shared humanity racket of winter deadfall between joy and liberty
It weighs on my soul like unwanted Snow Days
To a sad child trapped in a double-wide full of winter arguments
Sensitive as mourners queuing up to caskets
We learn to side-step one another hitching masks up looking down
As we walk down busy aisles and book stacks
Increasing our pace like scads of park geese or coots
Fleeing children released from the leash of parental control
Or as if the next soul elbow-wise was on their way to transforming
Into whirlpool maelstrom of churn and swamp gas a collapsing star's
Threat of gravitational pull and coal-sack currents
I wish I could get used to distance arrows and the canned purr
Of audio admonitions every several minutes
On the other hand when I see a young cashier's mask slip
And they pause to smile back at a customer before reaching up to
Guiltily tug it back in place (with a furtive check)
It seems like the overwhelming warmth of that simple sweet act
Is brighter than a thousand Siberian Tunguska Explosions

IF SAINT FRANCIS PREACHED TO THE ANIMALS

I have heard the tales about Saint Francis of Assisi
Teaching scripture to the beasts and preaching sermons to the birds
He is after all the Patron Saint of Animals
Sometimes I wonder how many interruptions from the animal kingdom
Might have ensued when he sat down surrounded by fur and feather
Tortoise shell scale wool and hide in some clearing enfolded by
The sublime peace of amber light shade and green
Because there's always one always one in every crowd

I can just see a shaggy brown bear rolling up on his haunches
Having dozed through most of the Beatitudes
His long muzzle girdled with deer flies and blackberry juice
Ears twitching at tick-bite scarred black nose snuffling
Maybe taking a moment to scratch his back against
An old oak tree's bear-scrubbed trunk

Then raising a catcher's mitt paw to the blessed saint
And in his gruff bruin's voice saying:

Sir, Titus is a great book but can we please skip back to Samuel
To the part where Prince Johnathan dipped his staff's point
Into the honeycomb and his eyes were enlightened
Or the Gospel of John when Jesus appeared to the apostles on the shore
And told them to cast their nets on the other side of the boat
And the nets almost broke because of there were so many fish
Or about the hills dripping milk and honey?

And of course a big buck with its sugar maple leaf-shaped ears
Turned its antlered head to a racoon
Across the glade and the two of them
Shot each other a look that said here we go here we go again

FALLING

I didn't laugh when The President stumbled
When he fell going up the steps of Air Force One
I felt pity for him and anger for those exploiting his decline
And I felt sorrow for all of us on either side of the divide
Because we're falling with him aren't we
Not linked-hands love and faith in sky-divers' communion
But bloody awful clown falls bozo banana sprawls
Drunk carny barker trips off the sideshow's platform
The firemen pigs yanked off their trotters by the short hose
Calliope cut-ups and tangoes through the deadly nightshade
Honestly none of this is funny worthy of hoots and popcorn
No more than the inebriated beer-can crushers
At a family function egging on their senile grandfather
To try his hand at his school jock high-jump win
No more than a bus driver leaving the school children
Lost in a mountain night of Slavic conifers and fog
Or the seeing-eye dog leaving his owner
Groping down the length of subway rail
I couldn't yell at him because I expected nothing different
How could I expect anything different from him given what he is?
But I wanted to scream at his wife his party his admin his handlers
(does he have an admin-does he have handlers)
The people who went to the polls and cast their votes
Do you see this do any of you see this
Really is this what you want is this what you want?

I wanted to turn on what passes as the press
Blind like splay limbed axolotls floating
In the night-silt of a Lake Xochimilco canal
And ask them
Is there one of you-just one of you
With
A
Shred
Of
Pity?

TUXEDO CATS AND COVID

I am stalking the limits of Covid recovery
While just beyond my kitchen window
In the backyard near the pool
A fat tuxedo cat is stalking morning doves
I think I have a better chance of meeting my objective
Knock wood and all that I sure hope so
Then Mr. Whiskers-Late-For-The-Recital
And as for the sand-colored drumsticks on the fly
The duo that usually stake out the fig tree
For their daily perch and palaver
They not playing along with the program
(the hummingbirds have also packed it in)
They are leading him a merry chase
Flitting from the dividing wall to the back wall
Determined to avoid being brekkie as Bethany would say
I am enjoying my lukewarm cup of coffee and the spectacle
Of Mr. Whiskers-Won't-Make-Curtain-Call's frustration
And finally after flattening himself like a snake and
Carefully shadowing them from one bit of block to another
He's tossed in the towel and is currently sulking
Beneath the planter's overhang of root-bulged brick
When a good chuckle gets me coughing
Setting off a new klaxon of pain in my kidneys
That's when he lifts his inscrutable cat's mask
And fixes me with his cold chatoyant gaze
As if to say
Go ahead and laugh
I lost two birds
But you're not out of the woods

WALK IN THE PARK 12/26/20

My twin daughters and I walked down to the stream's edge
They hunkered down on the grass while I kept my feet
Victoria's over-packed backpack easy on my shoulder
And we watched the white egret and the soot-colored whimbrel
Stilt-walk through the narrow brackish trough
Like a couple ministers looking for a congregation's secret sins
Or light and dark angels observing an interminable truce
Stabbing/dipping their beaks down when they found
A good morsel of water bug or plant
Gold-black doubloons of mid-afternoon light
Flowing over their feathers oblivious to us
When we continued down the trail
We stopped to gander at a single black cormorant
Nailed to a desiccated thrust of winter pine
Overlording a patch of reed-mat and lake slime
The salt-stained head tilted up at a questing angle
The merciless eye and hooked beak nailing us where we stood
Seeming to find the day's weak denim sky wanting
Like a schoolteacher waiting for a slow child to
Produce the right answer to the question he posed

BEST SERVED COLD

Matthew 24:12 English Standard Version (ESV)

"¹² And because lawlessness will be increased,
the love of many will grow cold."

I read the awful news story of the young man who held on to
A video posted four years ago by an acquaintance
A young woman who said the N Word on camera
Later when she was accepted by the school of her dreams
The youth decided to release the film
In the hopes of destroying her life and reputation
In the hopes of denying her the prize (he succeeded)
Of a place on the cheer-squad she was looking forward to
Never stopping to think whether it was just stupid youth
Bound to be repented come hindsight and time
Never stopping to think that it would come back to haunt him
It was a dish the young man believed best served cold
And once again I found myself despairing of a world
Cold as a patch of arctic tundra or field of winter stubble
Overhung by pewter skies and crow funnel
God and mercy and forgiveness no more than a
Fumbling breeze at the broken window of a tar-paper shack
The better angels of our nature wing-sheared by malice

Then I remembered the young girl who created teddy bears
To comfort the orphaned children of police offers fallen in duty
Bears dressed in the scraps of their parents' uniforms
The Fayette County man who at age 94
Still makes wooden Christmas toys for the kids
The police officer who adopted the abused child
He had rescued during a 911 call
I thought about the missionaries bringing God's Word

Food bedding and schoolbooks to the needy
In every clime and corner of this benighted world of green and gold
Wondering how they would square their bills next quarter
I remembered good teachers paying for school materials
Out of their own pockets despairing over Common Core
And too many desks and too little time
I thought about the caregivers who bring groceries
To veterans who see IEDs under every car
The doctors and nurses putting in long hours in the Covid wards
Arriving home in the dark to trail fingers over
A sleeping child's face before finding their beds

And I forgot the mole-blind justice of the perpetually outraged
The merciless children of Cancel Culture and university
Their blind battalions of entitlement and rage
Their plastic anarchy shields and caustic cocktails
The pettiness of the lean souled and Woke
And I remembered the morning reveille of good hearts
Charity bright as the ingot gleam of a hummingbird's throat
Or Japanese fire maples at dusk
I rejoiced because simple decency still abounds
That even as the noonday dark of mean days increases
Compassion persists like a thread of thrush and wren song
Between rainfall and sleet a fond dream of fishes and loaves

I thanked The Lord for kind-hearted people everywhere
In Baton Rouge Beijing Sofia or Fallujah
For people who can still find forgiveness in their hearts
Nursing a sliver of the dogwood cross
Into new wood and green fig
For people who believe in a new slate
The ability to shake off Damascus dust and
To look into the depths of a scuffed and mottled mirror
And see the plea of someone somewhere
For a second chance

DRONE-STRIKE

When the woman reporter on MSNBC suggested drones
Be employed to remove Trump supporters (insurgents)
I found myself reflecting on Jesus Christ's denial of a
God-Fire call by the apostles James and John
Against the Samaritan village that denied The Lord hospitality
And I remembered the rebuke that stilled the itchy fingers
That wanted to turn the sky into a roiling skrim of fire and brimstone
I recall the words I came to save men not to destroy them
Those words doused anger and pride of those two like a bucket of
Winter well water a swift housing off of high dudgeon
The way Abigail lighted off the ass and calmed David down
When he was ready to wipe out Nabal for a lack of gratitude
The return to sputtering gasping blowing sanity
Back to drenched stiff-legged dripping perspective
And I reflected here as we are in these merciless times
Social-media beat-downs and burn-downs incendiary words
Magma-hot rivers of endless and acrimonious threads
The tongues smoking arrows falling 24/7
I yearned for soft rains ice-water down mountain corniches
The high-impact blast of firetruck cannons on crowd violence
A quick wipe-out in emerald wave and spume
Even in a pinch a clown's squirt-button spray
(chill out chill out you need to chill out)
Good fireman on ladders reaching for kids through fuming glass
Volunteers moving through crackling spruce to bucket off blazes
I thought of Christ who could have called in His own drone-strike
Right there before Pilate's throne when The Author of Life
Was surrounded by the Pharisees and people howling for His death
So as I read the reporter's words and expressed approval by pundits
For a quick erasure of strangers by fire or bullet
I wished beyond wishing that they could hear
The voice of The Coming King

Soft as a summer shower cool as cottonwood shade by a river's edge
Washing off the old skin of tribalism like Naaman's leprosy
In the refreshing balm of the river Jordan
Asking:
Do you know what manner of men you are?
Do you know what manner of men you are?
Do you?

BORDER WALL/EL PASO, TEXAS MARCH 30, 2021

I watched the footage of human traffickers dropping the two little girls
Over the US-Mexico border wall my mind and eye beggared by
The chiaroscuro of dark earth and infrared gray of bodies and wall
I watched in disbelief the hoist and suspension of form
As the oil-patch dogs of the inexpressible
Went about their service maintaining the machinery of night
The adamantine grind of dragon scale on dragon scale
I watched one child fall and then the other
Landing rump-first in the dust and sand
Abandoned to the corrida of scorpion snake coyote puma
The tender mercies of night cold moonlight and scrub
The thin milk of the indifferent stars
And as I watched the traffickers run back towards the hills
(the kids were rescued soon after by the border patrol)
Gray ghost-smears on video heat signatures without human warmth
I found myself wondering about their first drop
When they left decency to sad gravity
Conscience a palm's turn of owl pellets
Whipped away into the dark

WHITE HERON

When I imagine the grace of the soul's passage
The blinding beauty of its divine egress
It's hard not to picture this white heron
Gliding with ease out of noon's stipple
Of shadow and light

REMEMBER LOVE

Remember love for The Lord don't squirrel it away
Like a rampant griffin or a crowned hart wrapped in ivy
Tucked away in the letters of a medieval illuminated manuscript
A half-glimpsed dream in a Thorazine patient's eye on ward-walk
Of a half-diamond dip and eel-shimmy of kite
Slipping past the corner of a sun-warmed institution glass
Refresh it like a bear doing a back rumba on a cottonwood's hide
Or a jazz band broken down on the roadside waiting for the tow
Jamming putting on the sets saxophone trombone bass and piano
Even if no one's watching but the warblers and the racoons
The good notes half-notes plashing the soul
like sweet water from the Jordan
Go to it each day like an inner-city spray-can artist
Working on a building mural in high summer's braise
Best piebald pit-bull buddy head-wagging tongue-hanging at his side
Raring for the work heart foundry fire-choir of gratitude
Internal air-conditioning in-step with steppe-cool
Ignoring the day's Viking hammer of humidity and smog
Sidling up to the stone and paint's testimony
Smiling at a curve of indigo grin and gold gull
Smelling the spices the perfume and the chrism
Breaking out in the first wide smile
As if to say
Our last talk was so beautiful
Where did we leave off?

ART IN THE PARK 02/27/21

My daughters and I stood on a park path's rise
In the cool of sun-dappled willow oak and eucalyptus
On the green knoll to our right next to the black wrought iron fence
Cutting off the park green from the youth sanctuary
Four girls in their late teens/early twenties girls sat cross-legged
at a small table
Festooned with art supplies and they were lifting up their small easels
Showing off their pictures a beatific smile on the lips
Of their leader her eyes dancing beneath a storm of
Chocolate pre-Raphaelite curls laughing with the rest of them
Pointing at a canvas here and there while the others
Responded with enthusiastic nods and peels of giggles
My heart chimed parted released double-helixes of
Monarch butterflies at the simple God-given/furthered
Gift of artistic creation no dudgeon no offense
No sea of furrowed brows following a fist's grail
Into broken glass and frisking firelight
Just youth having a go with brush and canvas
Trying to capture the fleeting miracles of verdancy and light
The curve of limb the cavalcade of mallard
I said a blessing for the sufficiency of such things
That laughter aesthetics friendship the volubility of young women
Could still be had on a lazy park day in February
I reckoned it a perfect moment a well-wrought rondel
Echoing back on itself out of an interstice of space and time
I said to myself this can't be improved on
Even if a thousand small terriers and corgis raced by
In dog wheelchairs mouths grinning tongues lolling

Then my daughters and I looked down
And saw the cherry trees in full bloom

THE MIND CANNOT PLUMB THE DEPTHS OF GOD'S LOVE

The mind cannot plumb the depths of God's love
The substitutionary sacrifice of The Son
Salvation for sinners by the grace of His shed blood
Grappling with the enormity of it
Is as easy as plunging a Canadian lynx into a tub of ice-chips
Or trying to ravel up Peter's canopy
It cannot be contained by apse chancel corbel buttress or altar
Church cathedral mission sanctuary
The fires of the empyrean cannot hold it
But maybe there are times when we can approach understanding
Instants of quicksilver recognition and realization
As when a shell resists the oyster-shucker's knife
The shell lifting sufficiently to give us a gleam of pearl
When human beings stumble out of
Their soul's masticating night of hate or dumb pride
Because someone heard that small still voice
Awake or sleeping some murmured half-remembered kindness
Like a terrorist unstrapping a suicide-vest
In the cell of his rented room
Because he hears the morning song of an Abyssinian white-eye
Just beyond the iron railing of his balcony
Or a prisoner disassembling his improvised shank
In the morning before his cell-block fight
Because he remembered the chaplain
Quoting Proverbs 13:2 and when he woke he recalled a dream
Of twilight rose parents and home
A spouse with violence in their heart breaking down
Because they heard a mother on a subway platform
Tearfully ask their child why do you do that why do you why
Perhaps a father relenting after an argument with their oldest child
Rising to walk into her room to place a copy
Of Dave Eggers' What is The What at their bedside

And saying very softly you need to read this
This is one of the most spiritually transcendent things I have read
Perhaps there are innumerable opportunities for grace
Surrounding us each and every day
Like standing transfixed in a storm of pigeon wings
Tourists by a fountain in a foreign country
Frozen in joy at the rhapsody of wing and sunlight
And one can believe in street buskers
Infused with the power of divine intervention
Calling us away from major catastrophes and minor estrangements
The language of regeneration contained in a sawing fiddle bow
And once again we can see the finger writing in the dirt
And hear the rocks hefted for a stoning fall to the ground
See the prostitute's tear-streaked gaze
Lazarus' cerements sloughing away
As he feels his way out of the tomb and into the light
Because of the immutable love of God

CRITICAL RACE THEORY

(Dedicated to Daryl Davis)

I don't think Daryl Davis believed in it
I don't think he subscribed to academia's victim speak
The black man author and keyboard artist
Who jammed with Chuck Berry and Little Richard
Plucked off the white Klan hoods with brotherhood
Surer than a raptor's talon a quail's head
The proffered hand of friendship did it
The courage to part the famished spirit's
Old strands of briar and barbed wire did it
He helped many make their renunciation of
Moonlight ride graveyard horn bullwhip and burning cross
The terrible faith of peaked hood and low mind
He found the right progression chords
Struck the solid note to stake out a singing Ezekiel pump
Of new and improved heart hollyhocks from granite
"How can you hate me if you don't know me?"
That was all it took those simple love-breathed words
Which helped a Grand Dragon shed his fusty old scales
Convinced an Imperial Wizard to hand over his robes
Words that turned a room in Davis' home
Into a museum of cast aside hate-wear
A gallery of old ghosts that heard the new heart
Open up like Saul's God-gummed eyes
And sighed and wept

THE ORANGE SELLER BY ENRIQUE SERRA (1908)

When I look at the painting The Orange Seller by Enrique Serra
Taking in the dreamy expression of the young Moroccan girl
Sitting next to her brimming plate of wares
Brown waterfall of tresses against a hanging rug
White stars scattered on a blue skirt
The faded blue of a bombardier's sun-narrowed eyes
One bare foot tucked under the other
I wish I could go into the painting and buy
Everything on the plate and say hey are you okay
And can I bring you a cup of mint tea?
I would really like to bring you a cup of mint tea.

IT IS GOOD TO HAVE ANOTHER CHANCE

It is good to have another chance
To get up and go to work like a brash centurion
With a new command under his belt
Resolve tethered to a lanyard of cuirasses and morning light
Un-clogging the sours and the darks
Out of yesterday's old and tired heart
To re-prime the pumps and ventricles
To rejoice in a new morning's brindles and blues
New wonders bright as the brush of an arctic fox
Hours unsullied rife with possibilities
What a pleasure to have another day
To be able to share His word with others
To call unspent kindnesses to the fore
Like a lost dog from a wind-whickered lot
Or a stunned child from a war-gutted hovel
Each morning we need to remember why we were made
We need to remember why He made us
To go forth and glorify Him to study and grow teach and learn
To lead others to Him and further compassion
The heart needs to be more able
The heart needs to be more able
We need to be better at loving
We need to be better at using our time
Before the wolf-nuzzled hours of this world's long autumn
Tries to teach us to forget

NEW YEAR RESOLUTIONS 2022

I don't believe in New Year Resolutions:
Deep down we know what we need to do.
But my Lord look at the new branches and leaves
On the old olive tree.

IF WE ABIDE IN LOVE

"So we have come to know and to believe the love that God has for us. God is love, and whoever abides in love abides in God and God abides in him."
1 John 4:16
It isn't easy flashing jazz hands teetering on the edge of the heart's landfill
Navigating through anxious dreams of warning flares and klaxons
Squalls of earth-mover treads and falling clods
But we need to assay morning's dialogue with sweet beam and rose
Seizing apostrophes of light from thunderhead and crow funnel
Like catching the laughing blue eye of a beluga whale
While it shoots through glassine sheets of northern ice
How do we know if His love abides in us?
When we spread the gospel and share what material possessions we can
Food shoes coats socks a patient ear and open soul whatever is needed
When we see the need for physicians/nurses/orderlies/irascible surgeons
In this world's broken ward of flying gurneys and trailing drips
When we are willing to be as open as an itinerant street busker
Striking the right chord to coax forth a profession
Giving our testimony in rainfall or sun's dapple
We need to keep our reunion with love and compassion
Whether we come on at a rush like a kid with a sled-run
Or a senior's meander to that beloved visage in a train-station's crowd

NEW YEARS EVE 2022

Looming out of the trench-fog
Of No Man's Land
The mounds and mounds
Of unbroken wishbones

CARROT AND CRATER

I was restless feeling cooped up inside
So I went out at sunset to enjoy the remains of the day
The warm breeze that made delightful snowfalls
Of the white prunus blossoms that line the block
The contrast of blood-orange poppy blossom and yellow stamens
But the gibbous moon (waxing/waning?) rocked me
With its boneyard braggadocio even as the last of the
Sun's light died behind the roofs across the street
A pair of gulls crossed its face the undersides of their wings
Filled in here and there with brazen fire
A glory of red-gold that would have made a Scandinavian thane's girl
gush
Then I look up and considered the full effect of moon shadow
And I swear I saw a rabbit in a sport's car
Sticking to my story-a rabbit in a sport's car long ears flying
Behind his head like the ends of a race driver's ascot
Speeding off to pick up his best doe for a dinner date and dance
He was running late and doing his best to avoid the
Moon rocks pocks retroreflectors and flags
They had a table reserved at the Carrot and Crater
One of the moon's two or three five-star restaurants
No mask and social-distance dining rules
With an awesome band plenty of room for
Slow-dancing tangos or a hoppity hip-hop number
I wished him luck as he tore across the moon's tilted face
Sure that his best girl was standing next to an outsized hole
Her nose twitching angrily her big foot sending up
Puffs and squalls of lunar dust

TWILIGHT

Standing at the end of the front yard's walkway
I watch twilight's ghost-coat of blue and silver
Darken with the rising thrum of the pre-storm winds
Clouds of deep indigo are sweeping in from the coast
And I glory in the imposing pincer movements of
Cruisers and carriers of imploding cumulus
Some last late winter salvos of rain and wrack
As ragged scads of corvids complain
With their usual batch of rust-can colloquialisms
That the day's receipts of worm and seed
Fell well short of hopes and expectations
(A brace of Canadian geese going by agree wholeheartedly)
And just on the other side of the street
The fronds of our neighbor's skyscraper-high palm
Bristle and hiss like the plumes of a Greek hero's helmet
Waiting for the first wink of holy Ilium's spears

SUN-BLOCKER

Do you really think He needs your help
I mean just tell me who made you a climatologist
(or virologist, nutritionist, economist, agriculturalist, etc.)
That you should butt into this party like some uninvited DJ
Mixing tracks for the right blend of light and earth
Filling the grooves with the insouciance of dust and dim
Because you don't think He's got this song
Of brindled sphere and beam under control
Believe me He doesn't need you to quash the heat
To come up with ways to drop the braise to a low simmer
Between dawn's rise and day's ebb God's got it down
Don't think that's so then step outside when the light breaks
Just watch Him crown the ragged mountain tops
With morning's new plaits of solar chaplets molten laurels
Stand in awe and see the streamers and boas of mist
Shaved off the serrated ranks of blue-green fir and pine
Belly up to the edge of an old cabin's cedar porch rail
And cogitate on sunset's phosphorous bleed
Between leaf and humus branch and bough
Of Japanese fire maple golden ginko purple ash Shumard oak
Get out glean sunlight's spatter on the backyard patio
Listen to the young finches singing their hearts out in the milkweed
The bluebirds and black phoebes trilling on the lawn
Stand on your walkway and watch Canadian geese and mallard
Heading east or south against robin blue and cirrus pink
Noon's scintillant net helixing off of breaker and wave
Spangling of winter snowshoe as it darts through
The winking gem-skin of winter drift and spruce
Gander the fleeting ink-flow of cloud-shadow across
Devil's Paintbrushes in folds of summer hills of ochre and dun
No really He doesn't need you to dim the lights and divvy up the shine
He isn't asking you to darken a third part of the day
That's never going to be your gig

BOUGAINVILLEA

When I see the bougainvillea's purple/red flowers
Slowly taking over my neighbor's garden wall
I am minded of the slow creep of crimson
On a youth's cheek when his mother
Mentions the name of the girl he's crushing on

CLOUD-GAZING

I sat out in the back while Maureen and the kids
Worked on Easter dinner Ralph Ellison's Juneteenth
Cradled in my lap as I decided at my leisure
To try to improve my cloud-gazing skills
Mesmerized I tracked a long shaft of cirrus uncinus
Resembling a partially eaten mackerel
Xylophone of spine and ribs wisping away
Against the sizzling scrim of robin blue
It crawled its way northeast with stately sloth
Transforming from fatally wounded fish
To Mongol or Turkish fire arrow
Seeking the eye-slot of a Chinese Mandarin
Or French Norman Crusader helmet
Or an Apache brave loosing flaming salvos
Into the enemy's sleeping camp
Two lazy gulls did looping briars of gyres
Providing it escort like a couple psychopomps
In the service to a deceased soul

That was when I leaned back in my chair
Taking in cloud traffic and sunlight's brindle
The balm of tree shade and lilting Monarch
And truly content beyond my ability to
Even describe the freedom from time and stress
I said to myself:
"This-this is a perfect moment"

That's when the thumb-sized hummingbird
At the top of the prunus tree
On the other side of the back wall
Perched on its reed-thin branch of white blossoms
Trilled a few notes until I looked its way
And turning its head so the sun caught
The igneous gorget of its red-pink throat
Said:

"No, that wasn't. This is."

FAST FRIENDS GREYHOUND ADOPTION

During our block walks the girls and I occasionally run into
The genial older fellow around the corner whom we know from the
FAST FRIENDS GREYHOUND ADOPTION advertisements
That are displayed on the back windows of his two SUVs
Not to mention the wonderful holiday extravaganzas
He sets out each year without fail on his front yard
They always fill us with appreciation and glee
We see him and his dog making the rounds about every other day
He's always muffled in heavy coat and sweater
Always flashing an ingratiating grin waving a welcoming hand
Masked or unmasked he is always in a kindly mood
He always has time to pass the time and jaw
Whether it is mid-day cerulean blue or twilight's rose and indigo
I have a hard time remembering his name but I remember Jules
His greyhound Jules brown and white thin as a rail
With the weathered white of aspen trunks around his muzzle
Brown eyes a-sparkle mouth stretched in a playful grimace
He strains at the leash ready for a head pat or a chin scratch
His owner informed us that the mandatory retirement age for theses dogs
Is five years definitely something the girls and I didn't know
What I know of greyhounds is pieced together from commercials
Some knowledge of medieval hound-coursing or
horny Bugs foiling that bad dog
Trying to come between him and that cute mechanized bunny lure
But I don't think Jules is retired not with that eager grin
That good natured tail-wag and leash tug not at all
He seems to say don't you believe it oh no au contraire
The bright racing muzzle and the numbered coat are gone
And I've raced the good race against phony varmint and sock
Over and over but I'm not retired you can put me in coach
And I wondered when Jules is dozing away in his happy home
Muzzle twitching maybe one leg pawing the air

Does he flashback to when he was a blur a fur-bullet on the outside track
Or gaining flank to flank on the inside bright number shining on his
back
Amidst the scrambled prime and composite
numbers of currency and chase
Feet sending up sprays of dirt sand and clay
The muzzles designed to protect from high-speed
head and tooth collisions
I wonder Jules
Do you have irrational nightmares of monkeys in loud jockey clothes
Whipping your back with their tails while one of their competitors
Tries to wrap their little hairy hands around your throat
Do you wince at the memory of shots
for distemper infectious canine hepatitis kennel cough
Are you dreaming about rolling meadows endless beds
of Shasta daisies and dandelion
Overlaid with the particle-heavy easy carmine of country sunsets
All the rabbits and hares dialed down to slow lope and scatter
Does your number and muzzle hang from a peg
Either over your basket or maybe in the kitchen
Wherever you are in your dreams Jules running ambling loping
I hope
You are setting
Your own pace

HOMECOMING

A little while and we have finished the hard slog
Uphill combat brawl through slide of granite shale dirt and bone
This age's tough talus and cliffside shear
Rockfall of fallen systems failed leaders strong delusions
Minefields of deer skull soft pit chalk rot and mole hole
Back-pack rucksack becoming light as sea-foam
Chain-lightning's chancellery pointing us Home
Bringing us bluffside to delicious wind shiver leaning green
Balm of feather grass' undulance and impress
Combers of Shasta daisies whiter than artic fox or snow leopard
Dance and whicker of branch/limb blossom/bud
Windsong whipping away weariness drying sweat pops
An angler's cast of evening rose and honeysuckle
Sundown semaphore of firefly glint and moon shard
Dove tabor meadowlark jay chickadee finch and oriole song
The syrup thick chirrup and tremolo of cricket and spring peeper
Scents of cider wine beer meat fish roast vegetables
And before our brimming/unbelieving gaze falls on the house
Holding oak/cedar/banyan/baobab/redwood/spruce/bamboo
Held by oak/cedar/banyan/baobab/redwood/spruce/bamboo
Family friends strangers milling jouncing laughing joshing on the
Wrap-around porch young couples sprawled on the grass
Talking low arms around each other pointing at cousins cutting up
Elders in directors chairs heads together walkers and canes discarded
Whirlpools of kid chase and dog chase
Before our eyes flick to the amber spill of porch-light
Gold of nostalgia and moth-buzzed windows
Before our ears take in the first wood-saw whangs and chords of
Dulcimer fiddle mandolin and guitar burr of radio static
There's the long table countless chairs/settings in the high grass
White linen cloth fluttering like cuttlefish in the dusk swells
The wavery mellow of lantern light cutlery's moonshine

Sure enough someone among the place-setters sees us
Smiles and lifts a hand to wave us onward
More hands and more smiles as darkness grooves the fields
As a burnt-orange harvest moon starts to clear the trees
Come on come on we're waiting on you where have you been friend
Those 'round table and porch from the doorway and green coming on
Beckoning/applauding/cheering us on like
we're the Prodigal Son coming home
Like Ruth and Naomi finding their way to Boaz' kind furrows
Free of the hardscrabble and homelessness of Moab
Like someone stumbling through their soul's city rubble
Through troop rush guard crush ambulance strobe and klaxon
Like a bird addled by war-time slipping free of buckled cage
Relief of dam timber and mud swept downstream
Half-running now juice of resurrection filling very tired cell
The old world's mulch slipping from shoe soles
As someone points to the waiting chair
While chain-lightning's chancellery flashes
And sighs
Welcome home

CONVEYANCE

Poets are just the mode of conveyance
That's what someone said (naturally) in a poem
The muse has already finished the work
The only thing poets do is set them down in print
I expect I read that in a Mary Oliver poem
If that's true there's room enough
On the autobahns freeways highways country roads
Off-roads and switchbacks of the imagination
For cherry red Chevy Camaros green Jeep Wranglers
Chocolate-colored Bentleys black stretch limos
Yellow VW bugs gold RVs battered sea-blue stock-cars
And red white and blue Harleys
Filling station just ahead
5 mi ahead at the next thesaurus
Mechanic shop 20 mi
At the next rhyming dictionary

SANTA CRUZ 05/29/21

Driving through the preternatural dark
Of Santa Cruz' redwood forests
I tell the girls to keep their eyes open
And check the gaps between the rusty giants
And the road shoulder for any signs of deer
That they might catch
Come the next curve smile curdling
I do my best to distract them
From seeing the deer they
Shouldn't see

I DON'T HAVE A PSALTERY OF TEN STRINGS

I don't have a psaltery or a Kinnor of walnut or yew sorry to say
My wife has a harp but the kids as toddlers 86'd a couple strings
And I'm not much of a hand with a tambor or drum
And pretty much so-so on the vocals if I am honest with myself
Which leaves me with the written word Lord 26 letters
A multiplicity of options exclamations fevers dreams regrets and praise
An infinite treasure-house richer than the gold wedge of Ophir
Wouldn't give them up for anything in the world Savior
Since you gave me the skill to use them as I will
I wish I could limn gratitude each day for your substitutional sacrifice
For the grace of the blood you shed on the dogwood cross
I wish I could write it with letters made of mini Glistening-green
Tanagers
Forest green yellow black turquoise bright
as Eden's vaunted vales and dales
Or the amazon's jungles with vegetation so green it is almost black
I wish I could put the words down as microscopic fowl and flurry
That even a back-sliding addict would put
the pipe down if I sat them down
And showed them the page I had turned out for your glory
If Salvation has a color and the soul's ultimate healing a hue
Wouldn't that be it-look at a yellow-bib pigeon tell me it isn't so
I'd be okay with the European goldfinch
face of martyr white daubed with red
How I wish Lord that when I set pen to paper I could lay down
The words in tiny aviaries the words singing a new song
Each and every dawn far better than mere feet stress and meter can
Letters limned in minute feather lifting off the page in chirps and trills
Salvos of song strains and tribute beyond
the day's gray burble of human speech
It would be a wonder beyond wonders to see the words and stanzas
Take off in the morn's first shellac of brindle gold salmon and red

Taking off fast as swifts and swallows through the white/pink canopies
Of the block's prunus trees or the pod-heavy acacias or green elms
Disappearing into the lovely scud of cumulus or cumulus congestus
Sadly that can't be so I have to labor like another old crow or grackle
Hopping about my writing desk scaring away the squirrels
And doing the best I can to keep the beak to the grindstone of muse

INSOMNIA 07/25/21

You never know what God will give you in the pre-dawn hours
Because you fell asleep too early and now here you are
Not desirous of food caffeine or waking the others
If only he could spirit us away to a seaside bus-stop
A clown this side of midnight juggling balls
A benign bozo with frizzed carrot-colored hair
Bulb nose/bulb horn puffed buttons keeping them going
Spinning a few plates now and then but please Lord please
Not insouciant enough to ask if you would like a
Nice coconut cream pie by any chance
Even as the gulls and terns complain beforehand about
The day's proceeds as morning light in rose and platinum wires
Snake their way across the sand and grit dusted concrete
Maybe it will be nothing more than your back patio
After a brief autumn rataplan of rain and no clown
But a single mockingbird sharing its love from the magnolia
On the other side of the back wall the moon peeping
Through back-lit combat fatigue patches of cloud
Or the back garage bare bulks splintered bench or bar stool
A fix-it or a chicken-wire skeleton made for something
Eagle's wing bison head daughter's profile heron bill
An ape in a top hat cravat and cane
Perhaps it will be a stint behind the keyboard
Searching youtubes for Scottish and Japanese folk bands
Sawing away with the fiddle working the accordion and bagpipes
The sudden Likes from your Scandinavian friends
Making it clear they can't sleep any more than you
Maybe it will be nothing more than sitting at a kitchen table
With the gospels or Billy Collins' The Trouble With Poetry
Your wife/husband's sweet exhalations coming from the bedroom
A strong breeze grubbing at the screen rattling the glass
And then the click-click of dog paws nails across the linoleum
Surprising a smile out of you and the good-natured query
Oh
You couldn't sleep either?

KYLE

There was something almost beautiful about it,
The purity of the impurity
The chutzpah in the eye lost to war-paint:
The call for the blood and bones of the boy
Who defended himself against the rioters,
When they waded in with firearms and skateboards,
The audacity and cheek of it took my breath away,
How can I describe the innervating hatefulness of it?
It was like standing in an autumn creek
Of water so clear and cold you wanted to cry,
Not minding the ice underfoot and at the shins
Because you couldn't take your eyes off
A single fist-sized stone
Orange as the unscuffed scales
of a Garibaldi

LAKE HUNTINGTON/11/15/21

I was walking the Lake Huntington Trail one morning,
Getting back to my regimen-taking advantage of the respite
From the previous week's lash of sun and Santa Ana winds.
Soon enough I saw that this summer's long pool table
Of baize algae had gone its way with the seasons change.
Now the open water was the ugly brown of Dinty Moore stew,
The long tobacco lanyard of an old hurt brought to light
Fueled by too much Jack and too few aces and hearts in the hand.
It was the dead seaweed brown of a bad dog's iris,
A big gum-furred stray winning itself a wide berth,
Giving off threatening vibes of incipient violence,
Like shivers of heat lightning over a field of June wheat.
It just seemed mean to me.
Mean, watchful and sullen.
Still and all, the mallards and coots and their dams were happy,
Though I missed the Egyptian geese and ibis,
The solitary white egret or blue heron that hugged the shore,
When everything was green and hopeful,
Making their way through the muck with glacial grace.
Not one turtle sunned itself on a waterlogged loop of timber,
Or paddled through the brackish expanse.
It wasn't summer-it was autumn-and this was an autumn lake,
Fug-ugly and opaque to the sun's weak light.
Even the towhees, the house wrens and western bluebirds
Couldn't put a good face on it,
Or the few tiger swallowtails and sulfurs that herked and jerked
Across the trail.

Curving around the far end's clump of trees and blue hydrangea,
I saw something bright flashing in the mud near the shoreline.

Beneath the briquet-black arms of the deciduous trees,
Stuck in the reed stubble and trash,
a mylar Birthday balloon of purple and lavender bobbed,
Like a Portuguese Man O' War washed up after a big storm.
And as the ghost of a November breeze made it ripple and spin,
It whispered forlornly,
I am Nobody's Birthday Wish,
I am Nobody's Birthday Hope,
Today or tomorrow.

PERFECT MOMENTS

What's the value of such moments?
What's the price for this glade?
This interstice of family and light's leaven?
This moment you bought for your children and yourself?
Earth's green hide staked out beneath your feet
Monarch butterflies in their hundreds
Jouncing and jerking overhead
Hanging like Christmas cards on tinsel
From the branches of these eucalyptus giants
The skin-sloughed trunks and stiletto-thin leaves
Crowding out autumn's sharp light
Cloud and sky's contract inviolable and sweet
As a couple's first long kiss
While you throw the frisbee back and forth
With your daughters
Taking a break from sketching tree and squirrel
The cool of clover and grass meeting your hand
When you miss the catch
A black phoebe singing overhead
In its cage of grass and twig
The loud click of a dog's nails across
The hiking path behind you
Reeds in the marsh shallows nearby bending like
Dozens of dance-hall microphones
In the hands of a crooners' platoon
The soothing sibilance of breeze and leaf
How do you pay God back for such moments
How do you not feel like a subway busker
Meeting the morning's reveille of bruised peach and tangerine
Pausing case in hand horn forgotten
Repeating to yourself I don't know where to start
I don't know how I can compete

TWEETS

2 Samuel, 16: 10-12

❧⸙ ⸙❧

"[10] But the king said, "What have I to do with you, you sons of Zeruiah?
If he is cursing because the Lord has said to him, 'Curse David,' who
then shall say, 'Why have you done so?'" [11] And David said to Abishai
and to all his servants, "Behold, my own son seeks my life; how much
more now may this Benjaminite! Leave him alone, and let him curse, for
the Lord has told him to. [12] It may be that the Lord will look on the wrong
done to me,[a] and that the Lord will repay me with good for his cursing
today."

If I could have had a moment of President Trump's time,
I would have sat him down and pulled out my bible,
And flipped through it to the 2nd Book of Samuel,
While President Trump did the same with his,
When King David, heartsore, soulsore, discrowned,
Chased out of Jerusalem by his ungrateful boy Absalom,
Refused to engage in insults, curses and bitterness,
When the clod hurling Benjaminite Shimei,
An old servant of gone King Saul and his line,
Taking advantage of the fall in David's fortunes,
Gloated over and harangued the disenfranchised
Son of Jessee-throwing bad rocks and patter.
Here was a hard-hearted pensioner seizing the day,
Feeling no pity for the loyal who followed their King out,
No pity shed for princes and princesses, wives,
For the concubines and the little ones,
Soldiers and foreigners who stayed true,
As they wended their way on the road to Bahurim.

Mr. President, did David lose his cool when the invectives flowed,
Like industrial effluvium into a sockeye's breeding stream?

When spear-toting Abishai, done with gloating Benjaminites,
Entreated his king to let him pin the hillside heckler to the ground,
What did Jesse's son say to that indignant warrior?
Remembering his own sins, Mr. President,
The weight of old adultery, Tamar's rape, Absalom's murder
Of the rapist brother Amnon, and the logistics of the next loaf and water
skin
For all those who had remained loyal, and above all, his faith in the Lord,
He didn't jump into the trench of the small-the mire of ego's dross,
But rebuked Abishai whose eye was on the hillside blot,
Rising and falling to throw another handful of dust and stone:
Let him curse, David said, if the Lord has put it in his heart to curse
David,

Then let him continue to curse me and maybe one day, God will repay
me
For the cursing that is happening now.
There was God's Anointed, hot and tired and turned out,
Of palace and ease, taking the fugitive's scrip and sack again,
As he did in the sad Philistine Days,
Large-souled, dignified-great in defeat in the Judean heat,
Bearing the abuse like a clutch of wet autumn leaves on his neck,
Giving it all to God, remembering with humility that indeed,
He was "a man of blood," and a troubled house was the inheritance
The Lord had promised him as the result of his sins.

Mr. President, it's never easy to walk away from slander,
To disengage from trading barbs and acidic ripostes,
There's a black joy to trading verbal body blows isn't there?
The bitter pleasure of biting into an Opal apple and finding a hornet,
It's an unlovely but thinly satisfying act of gourmandizing
On the rank vittles laid out on the plate of put-downs.
King David had lost everything. The foxes had their burrows,
The birds had their nests, but the Son of Jesse didn't know,
Where the dusty wend to Bahurim would end.

But he put a lock on the mouth and said the spear wouldn't fly,
Even as the dim little man capering on the mount,
Like an ill-humored Capuchin monkey,
Bent down to scoop up another handful of sand and pebble.
Mr. President, whatever dust Shimei rained down,
Was nothing compared to the dirt that David drizzled,
On the locks that had received the chrism from God,
The pencil-thin avalanche of dust that his inward soul
Let fall on his brow, remembering the evil days,
And that kings and beggars all fall short.

How it must have hurt, Sir-to swallow the anger and loss,
Not knowing what the morrow would bring,
The glittering tendril of dependents on his heels,
When a single word-the weary assent of a hand,
Would have sent Abishai clinking forward in his hot, dirty mail,
Launching a weaver's beam of cure at the grief he didn't need.
He remembered lying cheek-to-earth,
When the stricken child's cries filled the palace,
He saw the message that sent cuckolded Uriah to the spear lanes,
Joab withdrawing so Uriah died before the Ammonite gates.
And now, here he was-far from his gates-his capital,
A vagabond-but humble enough to find mercy in his heart,
To trust in the Lord whatever may come.

Mr. President, I appreciate your time, and I hope you see,
There is a time to speak and to bridle the tongue,
That a heart undone by anger and rage is a heart undone,
That there is a time to step away from the keyboard instead of
Launching a stream of sour spear-slinging Abishais,
Courtesy of Twitter and Facebook.
Rash words can have unforeseen results, Sir.
If I could have had a moment of your time,
To read this part of 2 Samuel with you in The Oval Office,
I would have been grateful for the time expended, Sir.

Maybe there are others who could have cut to the chase,
And simply talked about the Apostle Peter
And James The Lesser's opinions on the damage done
By an uncurbed tongue-I won't deny that, Sir.

You fought for your us like a centurion.
I often call you King Jehu, Mr. President: he was a king
Of the northern kingdom of Israel-Samaria-when it split into two,
And he got some good commissions completed,
Though he was a bloodthirsty bastard who didn't remove
The golden calves at Dan and Bethel.
But Mr. President, these days, we're more apt to get a Jehu in this country,
Then a King David, King Josiah or King Hezekiah.
And at least I never called you King Ahab, Sir,
A name that I have saddled your successor with,
From the very day that he replaced you, and he has earned it,
Every bit of it-he has earned it with interest.

Again, thank you for your time, Mr. President,
And thank you for all you have done for America.

I just wish you had considered your words a bit more.

WAUKESHA

When the man who drove the SUV
Into the Christmas parade in Waukesha, Wisconsin,
Killing six, including children, and injuring sixty-two,
said in his first jailhouse interview,
That he felt that he was being dehumanized and demonized,
It seemed to me that a bit of Tribulation's noonday dark
Had arrived a little early,
That the love of man-growing cold-was being cut with fentanyl
By some tireless cartel of gleeful demons.
The murderer just couldn't understand it:
Even his mother wouldn't drop by to visit.

INEXPLICABLE

Though we sit in our homes wide-eyed, treed like lemurs
Watching night's moon-silvered freight of claws and maws rumble by,
On the jungle floor like a determined column of legionnaires,
Though we grapple with the horrors of Waukesha and Oxford High,
Shocked that someone could commit the impersonal obscenity
Of plowing an SUV through a Christmas parade-killing
children and the elderly,
Or go to school and empty a clip into their fellow students,
Though we watch new atrocities push their way up through the
Nightsoil and mulch of verdigris minds, bloody and bright as Dutch
tulips,
Our brains balking, like a driver shouldered by drunk-points or bad fog,
Hands frozen to the steering-wheel, eyes shut by miles of shattered
strobes,
Even as we reel at the Law hamstrung and null,
Low-bailing and no-bailing human monsters into the shared light,
Blinking their way to disaster like moles turned out of root and earth,
Still, we remember the beautiful inexplicability of God's Love,
That wipes out the day's dark deeds like a sun's sudden nova,
When the Godhead, fingers freshly dabbed with the scales, feathers and
hides,
Bearing the palette stains of heaven's stones of fire,
Said Let us create sentient beings in our image,
We will have to die (briefly) as The Son to do this,
We will have to wrap ourselves in the lineaments of death for a moment,
But let us make Man in our own image.

Though the shape of the stipes and patibulum waver in and out
Behind the scintillance of new nebulae, gas giants,
quasars and constellations,
Grow as the first four petals of crucifixion's dogwood
greeted fresh sun/shade/rain,

(We will go ahead and plant the dogwood in our garden-we
will love the dogwood)
Sun spatter bright as ingots waking Adam
as he clears his eye of sleep's first grit,
Transfixed and kissed by the first songs of tanager, quetzal and goldfinch,
The air laced with the first tremolos,
buzzes and chirrups of cricket and cicada,
Their carapaces shining like a grail knight's armor,
Dazzled by the tourmalines, jaspers, sapphires and
jacinth of young dragon scales,
Groped to a sitting position as the stretched muzzles
of bear and jaguar prod
The outstretched hand bear/wolf/ferret/ram/lamb/deer mind wondering
What have we here what have we here just what have we here???
Brought to consciousness by the first perfect zephyr,
Fragrance of roses, lilies, daisies, marigolds, blossoms without number,
Even as we see all this,
And know the price to be paid resting in the dogwood's skin,
Let us.

BLACK HAWK

When I saw the footage of the Taliban soldier
Dangling from one of our abandoned dragons,
Ineffectually trying to change an Afghan flag for one of theirs,
That's when it slammed home-our fall, fall before all,
The Sad Superpower going down at King Ahab's command.
Here was an Adrianople fumble-a collapse of Roman horses,
Here was the wind whistling through the holes
In the arrow-riddled wolfskin tacked up between marble columns.
Here was the legionnaire's helmet bubbling up porridge
Over a dying fire in a pine wood fog, shield and allegiance shed.
Mission, Honor, Accountability, Allies,
Cast-off, abrogated, all sense springing away like a roebuck's ass,
Into dun and brown heat-shimmered hills,
War's rotors and motors wheels wings and ordnance,
Handed over to the bare minimum of anthropoid.

And the ghosts of the 20 years dead asked
For this for this was it all for this?

LAZARUS

⁴³ When he had said these things, he cried out with a loud voice, "Lazarus, come out." ⁴⁴ The man who had died came out, his hands and feet bound with linen strips, and his face wrapped with a cloth. Jesus said to them, "Unbind him, and let him go." Gospel of John 11: 43-44.

When he was plucked off-purloined from heaven's golden streets,
Moved back into Mid-Light Crisis and earth's parched grace
Like a man forced to do laps in an old-fashioned Bell's diving suit,
Shed of grave cerements and the scents of aloe, spice and myrrh,
Moving through real time instead of tomb time
at the command of The Son of God,
The new wine poured back into the old skin,
the new patch sewn on an old cloth,
The dust re-dusted and thrusted back into
the afternoon's Levantine bustle,
How did Lazarus deal with the day's poetry
of green shoots and dying figs,
The freefall of bloom, the mother and midwife's sobs, the baby's squalls,
The street bleat of rams and goats,
the rattle of Roman cuirass and scutum,
The hard-hearted arguments over coins and produce,
The olfactory avalanche of milling body sweat and donkey skat?
How did the day wind down for the returnee after the Lord moved on?
"Unbind him and let him go": but after unbound and gone, what then?
Returned to the hard business of living,
how did he adjust to the loss of heaven,
Deprived of The Light, praise rising and
falling like endless tides/cicada song,
Fellowship, service, preaching, holiness,
beauty without exhaustion without end,
How do you go from celestial emeralds and
jaspers to rough stone and weary bone?

("unbind him and let him go")

How about the crowd, jaded with miracles like cynical bombardiers,
Who have flown too many missions to be moved
by the prospect of death,
Insouciant after watching the lepers and lame healed, demons cast out,
Like bad renters bum-rushed with their eviction notices in hand,
The sight of the blind restored, the multitudes fed.
Once the revenant entered his home, did the crowd leave a few gawkers
To haunt the window and lintel and report if he proved voluble,
Shared the secrets of the next world, joys and secrets of the third heaven?
Did they haunt the yard and the lintel throughout the night,
Or at least assign someone (kids have plenty of energy)
To see if anything meaningful came from the revenant's lips,
Or to see if the mundane came back to the jump-started mind:
Does he eat, drink, remember his old debts,
the price of dates and grapes?
Did the young girl wonder if he had seen her deceased mother,
Was the Pharisee hoping he hadn't met his old mistress,

Was the centurion undecided if he should ask about old comrades?
I don't know. Eventually awe and conjecture give way to the need
To give the baby suck, to close up the stall and put away the wares,
To feed the family, to go out and carouse, stay up with the sick calf.
Maybe the wife with breat-cares,
turned in the night to her husband and said,
I do not feel right living on the same street with him,
Only to have her husband sleepily pat her hand and say,
don't worry, Miriam,
Eventually everyone goes back to the dirt-and maybe he wasn't dead.
Ha! You know that *he* can do miracles, so why not this?
Well, as long as your mother is living with us I can stand a dead man
Living a few doors down from us.

("unbind him and let him go")

Did Lazarus settle in with his sister over the evening meal,
Sclera, pupil, iris-wiped/scraped/bleached
of the holy berm's coruscant ways,
Fixed now on the indigo or deep green of the lentil bowl's rough wood,
The imperfection of the chip in the drinking cup's handle
(there we are back to everyday imperfections and flaws again)
The soot-colored length of the ladle,
the brown of bread crust, yellow of cheese,
The crease in the elbow, the scab's hill, blood's hum and cooling palm,
The blurry bug-stumble on the carpet or
swift window pass of pigeon wing,
The eel-ripple of cobweb in the ceiling corner.
Did he sit unmoving, lifting a spoon of lamb and lentils now and then,
Remembering sustenance and relishing food odor,
then setting it down in the bowl,
Not minding the spatter on bare skin, the inconsequential brief burn.
Was his mind a tabula rasa-the incandescence and knowledge of afterlife
brushed away,
Because wouldn't it be too cruel to go on
with total recall of divinity's realm.
When twilight made the transition from desert violet and rose to
nightfall,
When the last of the warmth bled away, fled away, replaced by chill,
When the brother couldn't just dab his fingers
into the dipping bowl of light,
Did Lazarus reach across the table and take his sister's hand,
Give it a squeeze soft as the wind coming down the burnt hills of Moab,
And say, I had forgotten night while I was away,
I had forgotten the way black and silver takes a land,
The long reach of the shadow on the ceiling and candle-dance,
The need for sleep, rest for the eyes and rest for the spirit.
Did his sister and other family members ask: do you want more light,
Did Lazarus smile a slow smile like sap slide down
a Kermes oak or almond tree,
And reply: it will be alright: I can hear the whirr of wings,

I can still hear the whirr of wings, I can still hear exaltation without end.
Tomorrow, I would like to sit in the sun,
And we'll see where we go from there.

LAZARUS #2

[43] When he had said these things, he cried out with a loud voice, "Lazarus, come out." [44] The man who had died came out, his hands and feet bound with linen strips, and his face wrapped with a cloth. Jesus said to them, "Unbind him, and let him go." Gospel of John 11: 43-44.

As Lazarus sat in the sun, moving his chair to stay in the light,
Watching the backs of the leaves transform themselves
Into swaying heaps of molten coins and copper ingots,
Counting the birds overhead as if summing the passage of errant souls,
A fly lighted down on the back of his hand and said
As it sawed away with its front legs,
Like an anxious porter only too happy to take up a burden,
Ah, good to see you are back,
Good to see you back, yes yes yes.
We had not begun to become friends.

CRYSTAL COVE 01/08/22

God playing His old snare
Tambour of time and tide
Uneasy meet of sand and surf
I chase my dreams of peace
And winter discontents
Back and forth in my thoughts
Like the snowy plovers
On this wend of wet shingle

UKRAINE (INCURSION)

It's not walking out onto the back deck of your country home,
And finding a happy bruin rolling like a log in the jacuzzi,
Or jogging through town at dawn, to find a Canadian lynx,
Eyes flashing green amidst wind-blurred grey and black fur
On top of an earth-scooper on the plot that will be
An upcoming subdivision sometime next year.

A flood of metal and boot soles across a border isn't a quick clatter
Of wolf-nails on the cobblestones of a sleepy burg
Finishing with the fast lope from a gleaning of glowing panes
To a teeming picket of winter conifers night and fog.
It's not like walking out your door to enjoy the sight of
Dawn's vermillion and rose raking the eastern horizon's grey bones,
And finding the pop-up of a homeless addict on your lawn.

It isn't a half-assed tanker's joyride to
St. Michael's Golden-Domed Monastery,
A truck-spill of lickety-split rifle patter in Sofiyivka Park,
And then back to the barracks with postcards and selfies to peruse.
It isn't a paper airplane's ghost-float over razor-wire.
It isn't some quick flashlight semaphore of skinned deer masks
Between moonlit boughs and moaning snowdrifts.
Do you have any idea what you said?
Do you have any idea what you said?

We can't walk back your words
like
Moon-walking Eurydice
Off the path of lyre's fire
Back
To hell

WAR AND EGRETS

I am standing on the park trail near the lake's end,
Trying to get my mind around the notion of war in Europe,
As my daughter, armed with her camcorder,
Is just below, stealthily negotiating the sun-spackled trees and brush,
Filming the snowy egret at the lake's edge,
Stick-still, white as a grail knight's shield, bill black as a drill bit,
With bright orange near its eyes.
Her sister (they are twins) is on the path beside me,
In love with the cream-colored retriever mix whose ear she is scratching
As the owner smiles indulgently and tells Bethany the dog likes kids.
Victoria is doing an awesome job as a stalker of egrets,
And later, Bethany will try to trump her by filming the briquet-ash ibis
When we round the lake and emerge on the other side.
Victoria is carefully negotiating the space between her
lens and the egret's fear,
The narrowing space between her quest to record
nature's beauty and grace,
The crucial feet between the bird's comfort and the need for flight,
The abrupt lift from the verge of water brown as French onion soup,
To the marsh area or another part of the lake.
My daughter is doing an outstanding job of ascertaining that moment,
And she stops about six or eight fee from
the waterfowl and gets her footage.
In her own way, I think, my daughter knows more about that border
Between her awe and eagerness to preserve
Nature and the creature's peace,
Then our President who said, disastrously, that the US would not mind
If Vladimir Putin's Russia made an incursion into the Ukraine,
Just as long as there are no deaths-but incursions
lead to blood, don't they?
They lead to the negation of national security and basic tenets of safety,
To the gut's cold clutch of fear and violation,

terror blooming like blue hydrangeas.
As I watched my daughter carefully back away, camcorder in hand,
Moving as silently as possible through light and shadow,
Giving a grin that she had captured her subject with a modicum of fuss,
Negotiated the unflustered feet between leans and wing,
I thought about invisible lines drawn in day's dapple and shadow,
And the fragile equilibrium of opposed powers-the
measure of earth and tensions,
The bat-speak of diplomacy/internet/media
descant bridging and inciting them,
I still could not believe that it appears that war in Europe is inevitable.
Even as winter yields its lease with these unseasonably warm afternoons,
The promise of spring's surety of life/
blossom/egg/womb/seed closer than ever,
Accompanying the glorious curtain-fall on contagion's
failed mandates and unhelpful masks,
How could the world back-track into winter dark,
black ice, reed stubble and mud?
As Bethany and the retriever and their owner made their goodbyes,
And Victoria gained the path, camcorder held aloft, her wide smile bright
As a band's brass section catching the morning's moot of solar glare,
I prayed that the world's leaders could defuse their hates and fears,
That somehow/someway, they could find that delicate balance,
Rein in the limbic lexicon of border and breach,
With the grace and forbearance
Of young girls and egrets.

SANTA ANAS

The big windchime in the backyard is going full bore
Gonging and tolling like a Buddhist temple bell
In the hands of a fuming abbot
Who is yanking the rope fit to kill
Because that young novice Yo out of Osaka
Who should have reported for the noontime meal
Is in the forest glutted with lychees
Snoring louder than a cicada storm
While he dreams of fox-witches
Leading him through deep blinds
Of summer green bamboo

BEIJING OLYMPICS 2022

How did you come by this venue?
What sorry miscarriage of sense, taste and humanity made it so?
It is as if a knight back from a holy quest sidestepped the waiting princess
To whom he owed a ruby of inestimable worth-the price of her ransom
From a brace of ogres or some lightning-fingered frost-bearded sorcerer
And tossed it with love to a black hopping goat with red leaky eyes
And castanet grin

JOHN KERRY 02/24/22

I read the man's words: how he deplored the fact
That the war in the Ukraine which had just broken out,
Might cause Vladimir Putin to not focus on climate-change,
And my mind recoiled in disgust and disbelief
like a sapling's limbs before a fire,
And-God forgive me-I gave way to loathing for them all:
The Masticators of Air, De-Animators of all animation,
The schillers for Gaia who can't give up their
planes and limousines and SUVs,
But root and snuffle for the slightest whiff of any plebian's carbon-foot,
Puffed up with self-righteousness like tide-tossed kelp bulbs,
Ignoring the child slaves who mine and labor for lithium batteries for
their electric vehicles.
I read your words while the Russian copters flew over Kyiv,
And for a few moments, I hated you worse than Vladimir Putin,
I hated all of *you* worse than Vladimir Putin,
As if you and yours were weed people grown in uranium-rich loam,
Some hybrid of half-melted sea lizard and
wiring on an atomized Pacific atoll.
A wreath of orange silly-string parasite in the heights of a senescent oak.
And I wanted to say: did you not see the interior footage
From someone's home of the Russian planes blasting by the window,
While a baby cried in terror somewhere in another room,
Or what about the father and his little girl crying at the train-station,
Before he sent her away to safety-and yes, here was another father,
Finger-drawing a heart on the frozen window of a bus,
His daughter-smiling bravely-reaching out to touch it
Just before the transport pulled away and he went off to report for duty,
Did you really think they were thinking about polar bears and ice pack?
Do you think Vladimir Putin is thinking about
climate change/global warmth?
Did you not see the old Ukrainian woman passing seeds

To the Russian soldiers on the street telling them to put them in their
pockets
So that when they died, sunflowers would spring from their corpses?
How about the young newlyweds Yaryna and Sviatoslav
Who said their vows and then went off,
AK-47s in hand to defend their land?
How could you have thought such a thing voiced such a dead-in-
compassion sentiment?
In what America nightshade realm
did you find the unmitigated gall and lunacy?
If it was your little boy your little girl being spirited away
To the bomb-shelter to a crowded Metro to some clandestine haven
Some secret place where you and your folk
go once the missiles were falling,
Would you be hawking windmills, solar panels and the latest Teslas,
Would you still tell us we had to do without their gas-powered autos?
When the shitshow of invasion comes to the Sad Superpower,
(because one day it will come here yes the
Assyrian will come here he will come here)
And it's our turn to hold the kids while the jets
scream outside and the lights flicker,
To dig out the guns from under the bed
or the closet and take to our lawns streets schools
Our turn to wait for the sirens amidst fire and
broken brick and sign up for plasma,
While machine guns chatter and glass sprays
and ceiling plaster and stucco rains down,
And the street rumbles beneath tank and troop carrier,
Will you or Greta lecture us on how it's sad that this is distracting us
From reducing greenhouse emissions?

TRAIN-STATION 2022

Waiting for the refugee women
On the Polish train-station platform
Struts flashing with the light
Of winter dawn
The empty baby strollers

SOMETIMES, IT IS REALLY THAT SIMPLE

When you are standing on the back patio at sunset
Slight wind whipping the blue hibiscus' blossoms
To a near-impressionist purple lather (called blue but they are purple)
The last sun-flints and shadow-spackle gathering in the cups
Of the South African daisies your chest tightens as you see
(you have watched them on and off throughout the day)
The slow back and forth of green army choppers of various kinds
Maybe no more than four at a time but even so even so
Rotor-thrum drowning out the quacks of passing mallards
And the honking of Canadian geese from the park
(one of your neighbors leaves bird-seed for them at dusk)
And you find yourself breathing a simple entreaty
Not to the conjoining of military might and darkening blue sky
But
To God
Each word compartmentalized and intimate
As a beloved's name spoken after a first date
Shared with nothing more than the long-dead light of winter stars
Or steam rising from a moon-lacquered auto's hood

You wish that only God and the stars could hear what you have to say
Because the words should be said not in the fading blue and peach
But to the few chips of diamond-speck lights
Stitched into night's black serge
Tossed off like bits of condensation from a sweating glass

You think of those going about their business inside the house
You think of the untilled work of the heart's affections
The weed-fretted avenues of stone-riddled loam
And as you watch the day's sad dragons go back and forth
You have to beat back an unfocused sense of anger and outrage
Going through your guts like a flume of cinder and ash

And you simply say
For them God for them give me another day
Let grow something good
Give me more time to grow something good
To take shovel to earth
To water seed

METAVERSE

You can keep your My Pretty Pony Knight
And non-binary giant cat avatars grooving together
In the virtual world you seem to want to foist on us
This sad slide into solipsistic coffee-klatch
Though I am sure that as war continues to bloom in Europe
And hope and desire wither here on the home front as inflation
And obscenity at the pumps continues to grow like cancer's metathesis
I am sure many will jump at the chance to flee this current reality
But honestly, I hope you will bury this bad and boggish dream of yours
In some muddy midnight patch of gator pen and hog-wallow
Shove it under the heaped-up gravy-brown mattresses
In abandoned field adobes off the highway side
Where addicts bivouac in their bunches and shoot up in misery
And please oh please sir just leave it there
Let's just leave folks with their "reality privilege," shall we?

Frankly, I can never get tired of God's old world,
Even at its worst, I want to immerse myself in it-jump right in,
Like the Syrian general-leper Naaman from the bible who
At the word of a little Israeli girl servant whom he and his wife cherished
Made the fast-track chariot run to see the prophet Elisha
(the girl in service said that the prophet could restore the general's flesh)
And at his instruction dipped himself seven times into the Jordan River
And the scales sloughed off washed off in the healing waters
The fish darting/gawping/unblinking eyes pop-popping
As the old skin sank or twisted in double helixes
Through the water's griddle of sun-shot beams and fish-tossed sand
Carried away swept away by the vagaries of current and light,
The new skin pink as a play-tumbled toddler's
As the general's attendants chariot-drivers and armor bearers
Shook like Parkinson's patients eyes wide as Horsefield's tarsiers
Stumbled back taken aback by the absolute proof of God's mercy,